Inequality Puzzles

1 Variable Word Problems

Fun Algebra

Princess Sasha Hides a Lion Family

by Courtney West, Ph.D.

For my daughter, Jazzmine C., with love

For my parents, Randall and Audrey Gaines, with love

For my siblings, Dawn W., Crystal G., and Randy Jr. G., with love

For my wonderful friend, Clay Holleman, with love

Dedicated to GRASP (Gang Rescue and Support Project), a peer-run, intervention program that helps Denver, CO youth stay out of gangs. GRASP's initiatives enable at-risk youth (ages 11-18) to be positive role models for younger children. To donate to GRASP, visit graspyouth.org, which is run by Metro Denver Partners.

12-Book Algebra 1 Series

Book 2: *Princess Sasha Hides a Lion Family: Fun Algebra*

ISBN-10: 1720333734
ISBN-13: 978-1720333739

Table of Contents

Princess Sasha Hides a Lion Family

(Pre-Story Algebra Puzzle)

Princess Sasha Hides a Lion Family is a wonderful story. I'll read it to you after you solve two cool puzzles. The first puzzle is called the Inequality Expression Puzzle, and it's shown in the red box below.

$$-3 < X \leq 4$$

The symbol **<** means **-3** is smaller than the **X** value (i.e. the number **X** represents/the number hiding behind the **X**). The **<** opens to **X**, so the **X** value is bigger than **-3**. The symbol **≤** opens to **4**, so number **4** is bigger than OR equal to **X**. The line (—) under the symbol **<** means the same as (**=**), so **X — 4** is the same as **X = 4**. To solve the above Inequality puzzle, you must draw the **7** possible **X** values for **-3 < X ≤ 4**, as shown on the Number Line below.

X values are **bigger** than **-3**   AND   X values are **smaller** than OR **equal** to **4**

The above *Number Line* shows an **open dot** ◯ under **-3** so you know that **-3** *is* NOT one of the **X** values. It shows a filled dot ● under **4** so you know **4** *is* one of the **X** values. So the **X** values are *bigger* **(>)** than **-3** *and* *smaller* **(<)** than OR *equal* **(—)** to **4**. Right now, draw *ALL* of the possible **X** values for the *Inequality* expression **- 3 < X ≤ 4**. Great job! Perfect answer! You drew:

-2 -1 0 1 2 3 4 and *solved* the *first puzzle*. The *second puzzle* is called the **X** *Value* *Matching* Puzzle and it looks like this:

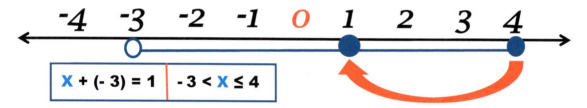

For the **X** *Value* puzzle, you must *solve* the *Algebra* equation **X + (- 3) = 1**. Then use the equation's **X** value to *solve* the *Inequality* expression **- 3 < X ≤ 4**. Fantastic work! You solved **X + (- 3) = 1** as **4 + (- 3) = 1** *AND* **- 3 < X ≤ 4** as **- 3 < 4 ≤ 4**. The equation's **X** value (i.e. **4**) *matches* one of the *solutions* (i.e. **-2 -1 0 1 2 3 4**) for **- 3 < X ≤ 4**, so you solved the **X** *Value* *Matching* Puzzle!

Solving Algebra Equations: 3 Easy Steps

To *solve* the *Algebra equation* **X + (- 3) = 1**, you used the above *Number Line*. You did the **easy things** below, and saw on the *Number Line* that **X = 4**.

2

1. *Find the equation's <u>answer</u> (i.e. **1**) on the <u>Number Line</u> and draw a* **large dot** *under it.*

2. *From the <u>answer</u> **1**, count 3 spaces <u>rightward</u> (for **-3** in the equation). You'll stop at number **4** (the value of **X**). Draw a* **large dot** *under it.*

3. *Draw an <u>arrow</u> from **4** (the **X** value) and stop at **1** (the <u>answer</u>). Then solve the <u>Algebra equation</u>* **X + (- 3) = 1** *as* **4 + (- 3) = 1**.

<u>*Algebra story:*</u> *Number **4** solves* **X + (- 3) = 1** *because a cat named Lilly had **4** kittens but **3** of them were given away to good families. Lilly now has **1** kitten.*

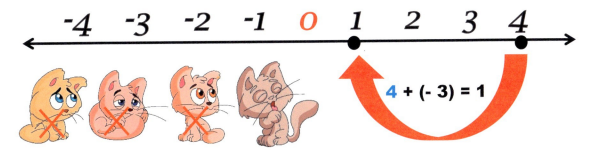

<u>*Note:*</u> *Negative (-) numbers (e.g. **-4**) are on the <u>left side</u> of **0**. When they are the <u>**second number**</u> in an equation (e.g. **X + (- 4) = 0**), count spaces <u>rightward</u> from the <u>answer</u> to get **4 + (- 4) = 0**. This Algebra equation also shows* **X = 4**.

<u>*Note:*</u> *Positive (+) numbers (e.g. **1**) are on the <u>right side</u> of **0**. When these numbers are the <u>**second number**</u> in an equation (e.g. **X + 1 = 0**), count spaces <u>leftward</u> from the <u>answer</u> to get* **-1 + 1 = 0**. *For this equation,* **X = -1**.

Now I'm going to read Princess Sasha Hides a Lion Family to you.

Princess Sasha Hides a Lion Family
(Main Story)

James was trapped inside an enclosure with his wife Lucy and their two children. Four-year-old Bryan felt sad as he listened to the father lion begging him for assistance. "Please release us from this terrible prison. We are so unhappy in here. How would you feel if you and your family had to live in one, boring room? You told me your father keeps a spare key in a kitchen drawer. Please get it now!"

Bryan responded, "I want to help you, but my parents will be very angry with me if I let you out of this place. I'm so sorry that my dad took you from a big, beautiful wildlife park in Africa. But I can't disobey my father and help you escape."

Right before Bryan fell asleep, he prayed, "Dear God, please help the lion family get back to Uganda. It's unfair that my father imprisoned them in a foreign country. They should be home . . . living in Africa . . . in nature with their lion friends. Thank you for answering my prayer."

As Bryan slept, a rainstorm began. Suddenly, a lightning bolt broke the lock on the metal door of the lions' prison. As soon as the door opened, the two big cats and the two little ones escaped from the nightmare they were living in. James and his family ran deep into the woods, far away from Bryan's house. A few hours after the sun rose, the lions walked into someone's backyard. It belonged to the family of a 4-year-old girl named Sasha.

Sasha was sitting in the grass between her two best friends Jazmin and Kristen. They were solving Inequality Puzzles when Sasha's dog Max started barking. The girls turned around and saw two ferocious-looking lions walking toward them. The girls immediately stood up and ran to the sliding glass door of Sasha's house. The lions quickly followed them.

Sasha opened the door and locked it after everyone was inside the house. Max stood next to Jazmin. He growled as two huge lions and their cubs walked toward them. Shocked and horrified to see the four felines, Jazmin asked Sasha, "How did lions get into your backyard?"

"I don't know," Sasha replied.

Kristen asked Sasha, "Do you think the big ones can bust through the doors?"

"I don't know," Sasha responded. The girls wanted to run upstairs, but they were too scared to move.

Max and the girls watched as the lions sat on the other side of the glass doors, only inches away. Then . . . the father lion started talking to them.

He said, "I'm sorry that we frightened you. We are very angry, but not at you girls."

"Who are you upset with?" Sasha asked.

"We are furious at a man who lives on the other side of the woods behind your house. He captured us in an East African country called Uganda. We've been living in one room behind the man's house for two weeks. Can you help us get back home? We won't harm you," promised the lion.

Kristen said, "The lion has a sad story, but maybe he's trying to trick us into opening the door."

Jazmin commented, "Yeah . . . what if they want to eat us?"

James persisted, "We don't want to eat you. You're the only people we know who could help us get back to Uganda. We want your help, that's all."

Sasha said to the lions, "Wait here; I have an idea." Then she asked her friends to follow her into the basement.

"So what's your idea?" Jazmin asked once they were downstairs.

Sasha replied, "Well I think I know how we can get them back to Africa. First, I'd like you to help me fill three bags with frozen beef. Then, if you trust the lion family, please help me take them to Gypsy's pony barn. I'll tell you about my idea when we get the lions in there."

Kristen said, "Okay, I'll help you. The father lion seems to be very honest."

Jazmin commented, "I agree, so I also want to help." After filling three bags with frozen beef, the girls returned to the sliding glass door. The lions were waiting patiently for them.

Sasha opened the door and introduced herself and her friends to the lions. "My name is Sasha; this is Jazmin and this is Kristen."

The father lion replied, "We're very happy to meet you. My name is James and this is my wife Lucy. This is Jeffrey and Jennifer; they're both three months old."

"They're so cute," said Kristen.

"They are adorable!" Sasha said as she held Jeffrey's face and kissed him on top of his head. Jazmin hugged Jennifer and kissed the top of one of her paws. Then the girls led the lions to a large, red and white pony barn.

The barn was empty, except for some hay and a big bucket for water. Sasha's pony Gypsy was in the animal hospital. Jazmin asked Sasha, "So what's your idea for helping the lions get back to Africa?" Sasha told everyone that

her uncle Paul flies to Africa every month to buy paintings, which he sells in the United States. Sasha then said, "Tomorrow afternoon, Paul will fly to Uganda in his airplane. It will be empty, except for his suitcase and some big boxes, which the lions can hide behind." Kristen asked Sasha, "Are we going to walk two blocks to your uncle's house?" Jazmin interjected, "That won't work; if people see lions walking outside, they're going to call 911." Sasha responded, "Well I have a plan. First I need to call my uncle Paul to ask him for a favor." Jazmin and Kristen didn't hear what Sasha said to her uncle, but they heard Sasha invite her boyfriend Joshua over to play. In **less than** (**<**) 10 minutes, Joshua arrived at Sasha's house with his friends José and Tim.

Sasha told everyone her idea. Joshua and the other girls agreed to help Sasha with her plan. José and Tim promised they wouldn't tell anyone about the lions. In the meantime, the children had a great time playing with the four felines until they had to go home for dinner.

The next day, the first part of Sasha's plan was a complete success! That's because Joshua used his toy train to drive everyone to her uncle's house. None of Paul's neighbors called 911 because they thought the lions were some of the children's stuffed animals. Sasha's uncle had a large, blue house, and behind it was a big, white airplane.

The second part of Sasha's plan went perfectly! That's because Sasha's uncle helped her with an **Algebra** problem shortly before his trip to Uganda. Sasha made sure they remained inside his house for at least (**≥**) 25 minutes. As Paul helped his niece with her **Inequality expression**, he didn't see the other children leading the lions to his airplane.

Sasha's friends and the four lions walked quickly to the plane. Joshua said to the girls, "Siri told me the flight to Uganda will take <u>less than</u> (**<**) 20 hours." Kristen said, "Good! That means the whole family will have enough food and water for the trip." Jazmin added, "Yeah, three bags of thawed beef and one bag of bottled water will be more than enough."

Once everyone got to the airplane, Joshua took the bags inside of it. He placed each bag on the floor behind some boxes. Then the lions walked into the airplane and sat behind the bags.

James briefly returned to the entrance and said, "Thank you very much for helping us get back home. My family and I are so grateful for your kindness. Goodbye." The children said, "We are very happy to help you! . . . Goodbye."

The flight to Uganda from the United States took 15 hours. Two minutes after landing in Africa, Sasha's uncle opened the door of his airplane. Immediately, the lion family ran out of the plane and into the nearby forest. Shocked to see the animals, Paul called Uganda's Wildlife Control Center. Two men (from the center) followed the lions in a helicopter to ensure they safely found The Lion National Park.

When the lions arrived home, Sasha and her friends were playing with three toys: two baby dinosaurs and a blue lizard. Sasha used her cellphone to hear a news report from Uganda. "Breaking News! An American man said a male and a female lion, along with two lion cubs, jumped out of his airplane. All four cats are now back at The Lion National Park." The children hollered "Yeahhh!!!" as they lifted their arms in the air. They were so happy that James and his family were back home.

Princess Sasha Hides a Lion Family
(After-Story Algebra Trick!)

Four-year-old Sasha has a boyfriend named Joshua. He's Chinese and wants to create robots that look like people. A big company will pay him lots of money to do this when he grows up. But first he must learn **Algebra**. That's because Robotics Engineers must have excellent math skills.

To practice his Algebra skills, Joshua is showing his favorite playmates (Jazmin, Tim, Kristen, José, and Sasha) how to perform a <u>fun</u> **Algebra** trick. It's called the <u>Inequality Matching Trick</u>. These <u>Inequality symbols</u> (i.e. **>**, **<**, **≥**, **≤**) are used for the trick. They show you whether <u>one number</u> is <u>bigger</u>, <u>smaller</u>, OR <u>equal</u> to another <u>number</u>. The only other symbol (≠) means two numbers are NOT <u>equal</u> to each other (e.g. **3** is NOT <u>equal</u> to **6**, so you write: **3 ≠ 6**).

Inequality Symbols: **>** **<** **≥** **≤**

Joshua showed everyone how **Inequality symbols** work, with these _expressions_:

1 < 3   and   **5 > 2**   and   **X ≥ - 4**   and   **X ≤ - 1**

Joshua told his friends that **1 < 3** means number **1** is _smaller_ **(<)** than **3**;

5 > 2 means number **5** is _bigger_ **(>)** than **2**; **X ≥ - 4** means the **X** value is

bigger than OR _equal to_ **- 4** (i.e negative **4**); and **X ≤ -1** means the **X** value

is _smaller than_ OR _equal to_ **-1** (i.e. negative **1**).

Four-year-old Joshua then showed the children how to complete the **5 steps** for
the _Inequality Matching Trick_. His girlfriend Sasha gave their friends blank
paper along with black, blue, green, and red crayons.

Inequality Matching Trick – 5 Steps

1. For **step 1**, Joshua told his friends to draw the _Inequality expression_
   -2 ≤ X ≤ 4. Then the children had to draw a _Number Line_ like the
   one below. They placed _large dots_ under numbers **- 2** and **4**, like this:

2. For **step 2**, the children drew a _line_ to connect the large dots, like this:

3. For **step 3**, Joshua's friends drew the *7 possible* **X** *values for* **-2 ≤ X ≤ 4**, *like this:* **-2   -1   0   1   2   3   4**

4. For **step 4**, *the children used the* <u>*Number Lines*</u> *below to solve* **<u>three</u>** <u>*Algebra equations*</u>: **X + (-2) = -5   X + 3 = -1   X + 3 = 5** *(see p. 2-3)*

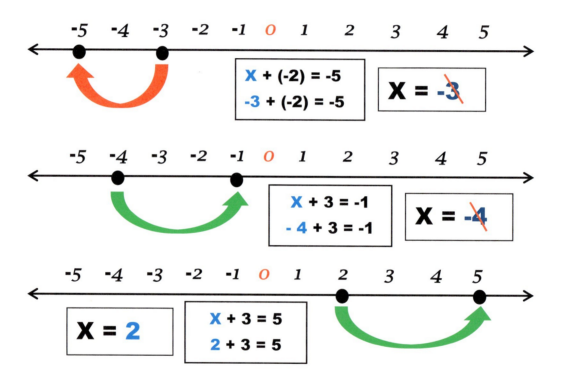

| -5 | -4 | -3 | -2 | -1 | 0 | 1 | 2 | 3 | 4 | 5 |

X + (-2) = -5
-3 + (-2) = -5

X = -3̶

X + 3 = -1
- 4 + 3 = -1

X = -4̶

X = 2

X + 3 = 5
2 + 3 = 5

5. For **step 5**, *Joshua's friends crossed out the* **X** *values* **- 3** *and* **- 4** *because they do NOT* <u>*match*</u> *one of the* **X** *values (i.e.* -2 -1 0 1 2 3 4*) for the* *Inequality expression* **- 2 ≤ X ≤ 4**. *They found* **X = 2** *for the third* *Algebra equation, and* **2** <u>*matches*</u> *one of the above 7 values for* **X**.

24

Right now, look at the **7** <u>solutions</u> (i.e. **-2 -1 0 1 2 3 4**) for **-2 ≤ X ≤ 4**. Number **2** *solves* the *Inequality* <u>expression</u> as **-2 ≤ 2 ≤ 4**. Number **2** also *solves* the *Algebra* <u>equation</u> **X + 3 = 5** as **2 + 3 = 5**. *That's why Joshua's* friends performed the <u>*Inequality Matching Trick*</u> *perfectly! Everyone found* **X = 2** for the *Inequality* expression AND for the *Algebra* equation.

Joshua and his friends enjoy using the <u>*Inequality Matching Trick*</u> to create *cool puzzles* for their parents, siblings, classmates, and each other. To <u>*create the puzzles*</u>, the children *draw* an <u>Inequality expression</u>. Each expression includes <u>one</u> OR <u>more</u> Inequality symbols (i.e. **>, <, ≥, ≤**). Then they draw *three* <u>*Algebra equations*</u>.

Joshua drew Sasha an *Inequality puzzle* (p. 26). *She looked at his* <u>Inequality expression</u> *and said,* *"I don't know how to solve* **4 < X < 104**.*"* *Joshua pointed to the first* <u>*Number Line*</u> *on the next page. He told Sasha that to the right of* *zero (0), the* <u>***Number Line***</u> *shows the numbers that* *can solve* **4 < X < 104**, *including 5-10, 20, 30, 40,* 50, 60, 70, 80, 90, 100 *as well as 101, 102, and 103.*

To get from 5 to 10, Joshua told Sasha to count <u>*five numbers*</u> to the <u>*right*</u> from *number 5. To get from 10 to 20, she had to count* <u>*ten numbers*</u> to the <u>*right*</u> from *number 10. By doing the same thing for the other numbers on the* <u>*Number Line*</u>, Sasha reached 100. From 100, Sasha got to 103 by counting 3 numbers *(i.e. 101, 102, 103). Sasha pretended she was counting rocks.*

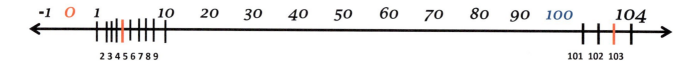

Sasha <u>*drew*</u> *the possible* **X** *values for Joshua's* <u>*Inequality expression*</u> **4 < X < 104**, *like this:* **5, 6, 7, 8, 9, 10-20, 21-30, 31-40, 41-50, 51-60, 61-70, 71-80, 81-90, 91-100, 101-103**. *Sasha saw that any number from* **5** *to* **103** *solves Joshua's* <u>*Inequality*</u> *expression.*

She asked Joshua, "How do I know <u>*which*</u> *number is the* <u>*correct*</u> **X** *value?"*

Joshua replied, "To see <u>*which number*</u> *the letter* **X** *represents in* **4 < X < 104**, *you must solve the* <u>*Algebra equations*</u> *below. One of the* **X** *values will be* <u>*bigger than*</u> **4** *but* <u>*smaller than*</u> **104**. *That number will solve my* <u>*Inequality puzzle*</u>.*"*

Joshua's Inequality Puzzle: 4 < X < 104

$$X + (-3) = 0 \qquad X + 3 = 5 \qquad X + 4 = 104$$

4 < X < 104 (**X** *is bigger than* **4** *and less than* **104**)

You can also solve Joshua's puzzle. Right now, draw _Number Lines_ to solve each _equation_. Cross out the **X** values that are NOT among numbers 5 to 103.

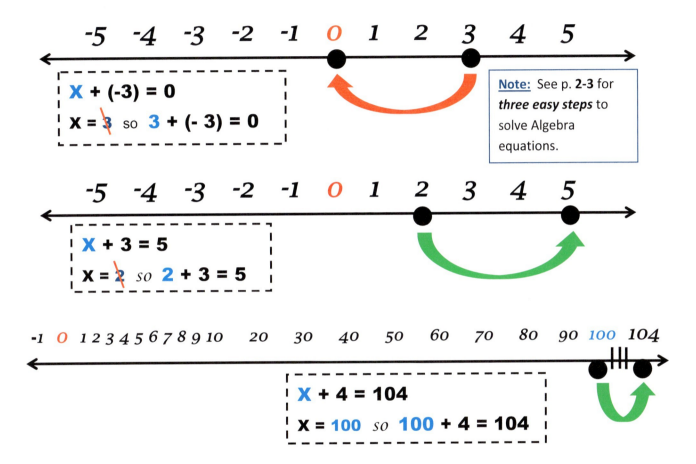

Terrific work! You crossed out the **X** values for the first two equations. In the third one, you found that **X = 100**. This number _matches_ one of the **X** values (i.e. numbers from 5 to 103) for **4 < X < 104**. So what do you _draw_ to solve Joshua's puzzle? Correct! Fantastic job! You drew: **4 < 100 < 104**.

Like you, Sasha found the **X** values for the above <u>Algebra equations</u> to be:
~~2~~ ~~3~~ **100**. She saw that on Joshua's <u>Number Line</u> below, the **X** values are numbers **5 - 103**, and number **100** solves the Inequality **4 < X < 104**.

-1 0 1 2 3 4 5 6 7 8 9 10   20   30   40   50   60   70   80   90 100 104

$$4 < 100 < 104$$

Above, Sasha *crossed out* **2** and **3** because these numbers are <u>smaller</u> than number **5**. With number **100**, Sasha <u>matched</u> the *Algebra* equation **X + 4 = 104** (solved as *100 + 4 = 104*) <u>to</u> the *Inequality* expression **4 < X < 104** (solved as *4 < 100 < 104*). So what <u>number</u> does **X** represent in the <u>Algebra equation</u> AND in the <u>Inequality expression</u>? Yes! Terrific answer! You said: **X = 100**.

Now, what do you draw to *solve* the <u>Algebra equation</u> **X + 4 = 104**? Magnificent! You drew: **100 + 4 = 104**. And what do you draw to show **100** is <u>a solution</u> for the <u>Inequality expression</u> **4 < X < 104**? Excellent job! You drew **4 < 100 < 104**. <u>Note:</u> <u>Inequality signs</u> always <u>open</u> **(>)** to the <u>bigger</u> number. Imagine it's the open mouth of a <u>bigger</u> fish eating a <u>smaller</u> one.

José Creates a Puzzle for Show-and-Tell

José's mother helped him create the super cool _Inequality Puzzle_ below to use for **Show-and-Tell**. Whoever solves the puzzle will see _how many_ frogs José threw into Sasha's backyard pond. José told his classmates what they must do to _solve the puzzle_. Then his teacher requested a **volunteer** to solve the puzzle in front of the class. Lots of children raised their hands, but José chose his best friend Tim.

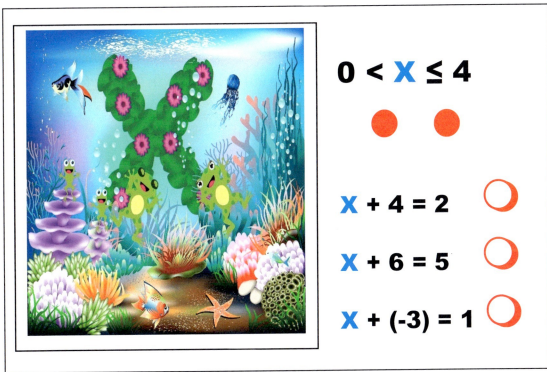

$$0 < X \leq 4$$

$$X + 4 = 2$$

$$X + 6 = 5$$

$$X + (-3) = 1$$

*First, Tim drew on the whiteboard the <u>Number Line</u> below. He did this to see the **X** values for the **Inequality** **0 < X ≤ 4**. Then he drew the <u>four numbers</u> that **X** represents. Right now, I want you to draw the numbers Tim drew.*

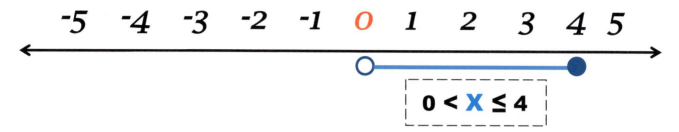

$$0 < X \le 4$$

*Correct! Great job! You also drew the <u>correct</u> **X** values: **1 2 3 4**. Next, Tim drew 3 <u>Number Lines</u> and solved the puzzle's **3 <u>Algebra equations</u>**. He looked at each **X** value and saw one <u>matches</u> one of the **4** numbers above. To solve the puzzle, Tim placed a red marble (shown on p. 29) in <u>**the hole**</u> next to the <u>Algebra equation</u> with the **X** value that <u>matches</u> an **X** value for **0 < X ≤ 4**.*

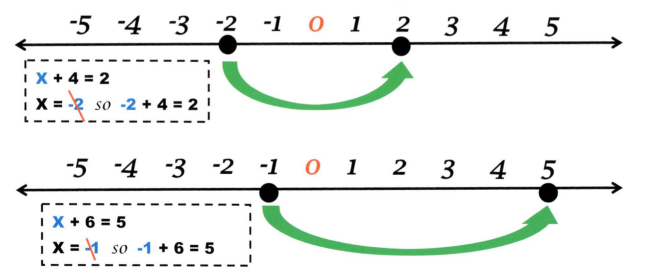

$$X + 4 = 2$$
$$X = \cancel{-2} \ \ so \ \ \text{-2} + 4 = 2$$

$$X + 6 = 5$$
$$X = \cancel{-1} \ \ so \ \ \text{-1} + 6 = 5$$

30

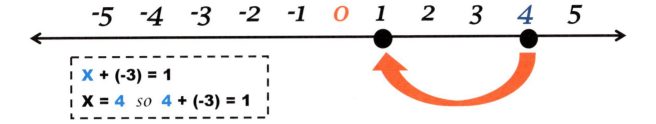

As shown in the above boxes, Tim solved **_three Algebra equations:_**

X + 4 = 2   X + 6 = 5   X + (-3) = 1

What are the three **X** values that Tim found. Perfect! You said: **-2   -1   4**

On the whiteboard, Tim crossed out the two **X** values that are NOT included in the **_four solutions_** for **0 < X ≤ 4**, which are: *1   2   3   4*

Right now, draw the equations' three **X** values. Then cross out the two that are NOT solutions for **0 < X ≤ 4**. Wonderful job! You drew: ~~-2~~   ~~-1~~   4

So what do you draw to solve the <u>Algebra</u> equation **X + (-3) = 1**? Correct! You drew: **4 + (-3) = 1**. And what about the <u>Inequality</u> expression **0 < X ≤ 4**? Great job! You drew: **0 < 4 ≤ 4**. So **4** <u>solves José's puzzle</u>.

As shown on p. 32, Tim removed one of the red marbles located under the <u>Inequality</u> expression **0 < X ≤ 4**. Then he placed the red marble inside the hole beside the <u>Algebra</u> equation **X + (-3) = 1**. By doing this, Tim <u>matched</u> the Inequality **0 < 4 ≤ 4** with the equation **4 + (-3) = 1**, and solved José's puzzle.

31

José's Puzzle

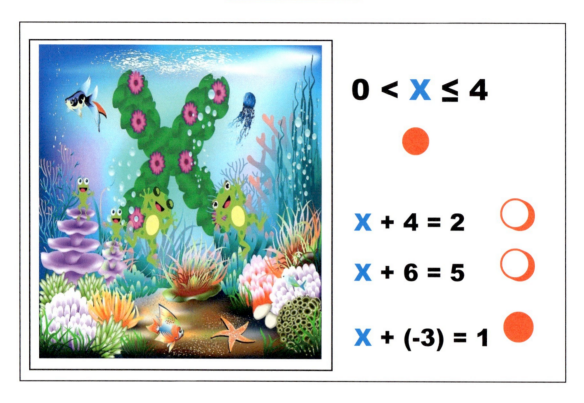

$$0 < X \leq 4$$

$$X + 4 = 2$$

$$X + 6 = 5$$

$$X + (-3) = 1$$

You solved <u>José's puzzle</u> so you know he threw **4** frogs into Sasha's pond. Right now, count the frogs in the above picture. How many frogs do you see? Superb answer! Not only did you say the <u>correct</u> number of frogs, you also *described* them. You said, "I see **4** frogs: <u>2 adults</u> and <u>2 babies</u>."

Number **4** solves the *Inequality* expression $0 < X \leq 4$ as $0 < 4 \leq 4$ *AND* number **4** solves the *Algebra* equation $X + (-3) = 1$ as $4 + (-3) = 1$. That's why number **4** <u>solves José's puzzle.</u>

Jazmin and Sasha's Puzzle

$$-1 < X < 4$$

$$X + 3 = -2 \qquad X + 8 = 5 \qquad X + (-1) = 2$$

-5 -4 -3 -2 -1 0 1 2 3 4 5

$$-1 < X < 4$$

By *solving* Jazmin and Sasha's puzzle, you will see how many **baby tigers** are at the zoo. To solve the puzzle, you must **match** the above *Inequality* expression **-1 < X < 4** with the correct *Algebra* equation. First, draw the above *Number Line* to see ALL of the solutions for **-1 < X < 4**. The **X** values are *bigger* **(>)** than **-1** *(so* **X** *cannot* be **-1**). That's why you must draw an **open dot** ○ beneath **-1**. The **X** values are *smaller* **(<)** than **4** *(so* **X** *cannot* be **4**). That's why you must draw an **open dot** ○ beneath number **4**.

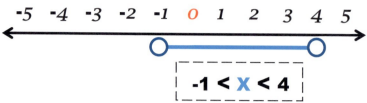

-5 -4 -3 -2 -1 *0* 1 2 3 4 5

-1 < X < 4

What are the **X** values shown on your
Number Line? The **X** values are *bigger* than
-1 and smaller than **4**. *Fantastic answer!*
You said the **X** values are: *0   1   2   3*

To see the <u>correct</u> value of **X** in **-1 < X < 4**,
you must **solve** these *Algebra equations*:

X + 3 = -2 *and* **X + 8 = 5** *and* **X + (-1) = 2**

The <u>correct</u> **X** value for **-1 < X < 4** will <u>match</u> one of the **X** values (i.e.
solutions) for the above equations. Right now, draw *Number Lines* and <u>solve</u>
each *Algebra equation* (see p. 2-3). **One** of the equations' **X** values will <u>match</u>
one of the **X** values (i.e. *0   1   2   3*) for **-1 < X < 4**. *Wow! Outstanding work!*
Your *Number Lines* look like the ones below.

-5 -4 -3 -2 -1 *0* 1 2 3 4 5

X + 3 = -2
X = -5 so **-5** + 3 = -2

34

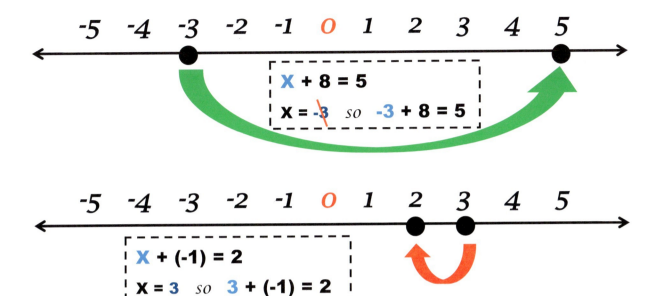

-5 -4 -3 -2 -1 *0* 1 2 3 4 5

$X + 8 = 5$

$X = -3$ *so* $-3 + 8 = 5$

-5 -4 -3 -2 -1 *0* 1 2 3 4 5

$X + (-1) = 2$

$X = 3$ *so* $3 + (-1) = 2$

*Your work is amazing! You found the <u>correct</u> **X** value for each Algebra equation. You drew each solution like this:* **-5** **-3** **3**

*You <u>**crossed out**</u> the solutions* **-5** *and* **-3** *because those numbers are NOT possible* **X** *values for* **-1 < X < 4**. *Look at the <u>Number Line</u> you drew for this* Inequality. *It looks like the one below. What are the possible* **X** *values for the* <u>**Inequality expression**</u> **-1 < X < 4**? *This time, I want you to <u>draw</u> them. They are located between the <u>**two open dots**</u> below. Great job! You drew:* *0 1 2 3.*

-5 -4 -3 -2 -1 *0* 1 2 3 4 5

$-1 < X < 4$

Never forget, an <u>open dot</u> ◯ under a <u>number</u> means <u>that number</u> is NOT one of the possible **X** values. Now, to solve Jazmin and Sasha's puzzle, tell me which **X** value for these <u>Algebra equations</u> (i.e. **X + 3 = -2** and **X + 8 = 5** and **X + (-1) = 2**) *matches* one of the **X** values for **-1 < X < 4**.

Perfect answer! You said number **3**! You are right because **3** is the **X** value that solves **X + (-1) = 2** as **3 + (-1) = 2**. And **3** *matches* one of the **X** values for the <u>Inequality expression</u> **-1 < X < 4**, which are: **0 1 2 3**

You correctly *matched* the <u>Algebra</u> equation **X + (-1) = 2** to the <u>Inequality</u> expression **-1 < X < 4**. They <u>match</u> each other because number **3** solves the <u>Algebra</u> equation as **3 + (-1) = 2** *AND* number **3** solves the <u>Inequality</u> expression as **-1 < 3 < 4**.

So how many *baby tigers* are at the zoo? You are correct <u>again</u>! You said **3** *baby tigers* are at the zoo.

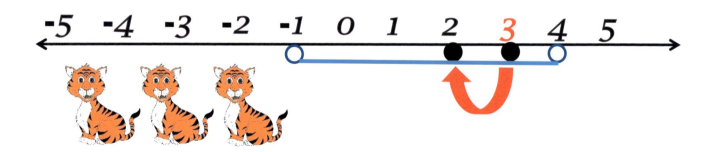

-1 < X < 4 *matches* **X + (-1) = 2** *because* **X = 3** *for both*

Kristen's Puzzle: 2 ? 4 ? 5

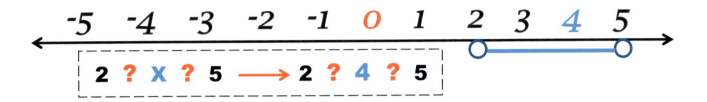

2 ? X ? 5 ⟶ 2 ? 4 ? 5

Sasha solved Kristen's <u>Inequality puzzle</u>. The puzzle shows **X = 4**. *Number* **4** *represents <u>four baby dinosaurs</u>. Kristen's Inequality expression shows question marks (i.e.* **?, ?**) *instead of <u>Inequality symbols</u> (i.e.* **>, <, ≥, ≤**). *To solve Kristen's puzzle* **2 ? 4 ? 5**, *Sasha had to <u>count</u> the baby dinosaurs below to see which <u>Inequality symbol</u> correctly replaces the question marks (i.e.* **?, ?**). *See page 23.*

On blank paper, Sasha drew the _correct_ symbol that goes _in front of_ the **4** dinosaurs (in first row) and _after_ the **4** dinosaurs (in second row). What sign did she draw? Yes! Fantastic job! Sasha drew: **<** Now draw **2 ? 4 ? 5** and replace the _question marks_ with the _correct_ sign. Awesome job! You drew **<** _in front of_ and _after_ number **4**, like this: **2 < 4 < 5**. This is right because **2** dinosaurs are _less_ **(<)** than **4** dinosaurs. And **4** dinosaurs are _less_ **(<)** than **5** dinosaurs. Also, **5** dinosaurs are _more_ **(>)** than **4** dinosaurs AND **4** dinosaurs are _more_ **(>)** than **2** dinosaurs. _Note_: Inequality symbols always _open_ **(>)** to the **bigger** number and _close_ **(<)** to the **smaller** number.

The **Inequality symbol** **<** _closes_ to the **4** puppies on the **left side** because **4** puppies are _less_ **(<)** than **5** puppies. And below, **5** ducks are _more_ **(>)** than **4** ducks, so the **Inequality symbol** **>** _opens_ to the **5** ducks, like this:

Sasha had a great time figuring out Kristen's _Inequality puzzle_. She invited her other favorite playmates - Jazmin, José, Joshua, and Tim - to her house so they could create new puzzles. Everyone drew _Inequality expressions_ with **missing** _Inequality symbols_ as well as _Number Lines_ and animal pictures. The children had fun figuring out the correct _Inequality symbols_ for each puzzle.

Problem-Solving with Inequality Symbols

Every Wednesday, Mrs. Baker gives 1 cookie to each of 10 children at lunchtime. Sometimes 2 kids visit her classroom, so there are 12 children at lunchtime.

That's why Mrs. Baker brings <u>at least</u> 12 **cookies** on Wednesdays. By bringing 12 **cookies** OR <u>more than</u> 12 **cookies**, she will have enough cookies for <u>12 children</u>.

1   2   3   4   5   6   7   8   9   10   11   12

The <u>Number Line</u> below shows Mrs. Baker brings <u>12 or more</u> cookies to class on Wednesdays. The <u>filled dot</u> ● beneath number 12 shows the teacher brings 12 cookies to class. The <u>blue arrow</u> from the filled dot shows Mrs. Baker brings <u>more than</u> 12 cookies. Together, the dot and arrow ●——→ mean Mrs. Baker brings 12 cookies OR she brings more than 12 cookies to class.

Below, **X** represents *cookies*. The sign **>** means **X** is <u>more than</u> 12 cookies. The equal sign – means **X** is 12 cookies. So **X ≥ 16** means **X** is 16 cookies OR <u>more</u>.

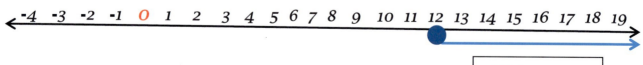

-4 -3 -2 -1 0 1 2 3 4 5 6 7 8 9 10 11 12 13 14 15 16 17 18 19

X ≥ 12

The **Inequality sign** ≥ means **X** is <u>more than</u> OR **<u>equal to</u>** *a number*. The sign ≤ means **X** is <u>less than</u> OR **<u>equal to</u>** *a number*. Look below! A <u>toy bird</u> was cut in <u>half</u> (i.e. **½**), so there are **2** <u>half birds.</u> This means **X** is <u>less than</u> (**<**) **1** <u>whole bird</u> (i.e. **X** = a **½** bird). How many **½** birds will equal **1** *whole bird*? Yes! **2** *half birds*! So you draw: **X** + **X**. Each **X** is a **½** bird, so you draw: **½** + **½**. So what do you draw to show **2** *half birds* <u>equal</u> **1** *whole bird*? Great job! You drew: **½** + **½** = **1**. Now you can place **1** <u>**whole bird**</u> on the <u>right side</u> of the wall. The <u>**Inequality**</u> expression **X** ≤ **1** below means the **X** value can be <u>less than</u> (**<**) **1** (e.g. **½**) OR **X** ≤ **1** can mean **X** = **1**. Below, is the **X** in **X** ≤ **1** a **½** <u>bird</u> or **1** <u>**whole bird**</u>? Yes! Correct! **X** = a **½** <u>bird</u>.

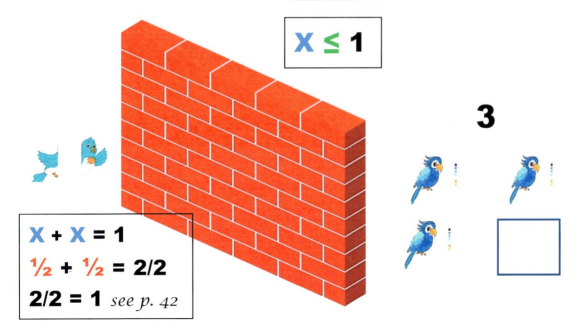

X ≤ 1

3

X + X = 1
½ + ½ = 2/2
2/2 = 1 see p. 42

41

Above, the **X** value is *less than* **(<)** 1 (*i.e.* **X** = ½) (*i.e.* *half* of **1** bird). To get **1** *whole bird* from **2** *half birds*, you must *combine/add* the half birds, like this: ½ **+** ½ Then, *add* the **top** numbers (*i.e.* the *numerators*/**1 + 1**) to get **2**. Next, look at the **bottom** numbers (*i.e.* the *denomenators*, shown as **2**). When they are "*common*" (*i.e.* **the same number**), you place *one of them* under the

added numerators, like this: $\frac{2}{2}$ *OR* like this: **2/2**

Finally, the *top* AND *bottom* numbers are *the same*, so they *equal* number **1**, like this: **2/2 = 1**. That's why ½ **+** ½ **= 2/2 = 1**. So how many **half birds** do you need to get **1** **whole bird**? Terrific answer! You said **2 half birds**. What do you draw to show there are **2 half birds**? Perfect! Outstanding work!

You drew: ½ **+** ½ And why does ½ **+** ½ **= 2/2**? Correct! Because you *add* the numerators (*i.e.* **1 + 1**) to get **2**. Then you place the numerator (*i.e.* **2**) on top of the *common* denomenator (*i.e.* **2**). And why does **2/2 = 1**? Correct! The *numerator* and *denomenator* are *the same*, so the answer is number **1**. And **1** means *one whole thing*. Now pretend the **X** in **X ≤ 1** equals **(−) 1** *toy bird* (instead of a ½ bird). Can you place **1** *toy bird* on the *right side* of the wall? You are correct *again*! You said, "Yes, because **X = 1** *toy bird*."

The **Number Line** below shows ½ is *smaller* than **1**. That's because ½ is *closer* to zero (**O**). Number **1** is **bigger** than ½ because **1** is *farther away* from zero (**O**) than ½. That's why ½ of a *bird* is *smaller* than **1** *whole bird*.

O   ½   1   2   3   4

So to place **1** <u>whole bird</u> on the *right side* of the wall, you must combine **2** <u>half birds</u> (i.e. **½** **+** **½** **= 1**). You can do that because the **X** in **X ≤ 1** can be *LESS* (**<**) than **1** *whole thing* (e.g. a **½** bird). The **X** can also *equal* (**—**) **1** *whole thing* (e.g. **1** bird). What do you draw to show that **1** *toy bird* was cut into **4** pieces? So there are **4** <u>quarter birds</u> (i.e. **X** = a **1/4** bird), like this:

Yes! Terrific job! You drew: **1/4** **+** **1/4** **+** **1/4** **+** **1/4** **= 4/4 = 1**
When you push the **4** pieces together, you get **1** <u>whole bird</u>. **½** and **¼** are called <u>fractions</u>, and they are <u>smaller</u> than number **1**. The fraction **¼** means **1** <u>whole thing</u> was cut into **4** pieces. Each **¼** piece is <u>smaller</u> than **½** of the whole thing. The fraction **¼** is <u>smaller</u> than **½** because **¼** is closer to zero (**O**) on a Number Line, like this:

$$\longleftarrow \quad O \quad ¼ \quad ½ \quad\quad 1 \quad\quad 2 \quad\quad 3 \quad\quad 4 \quad\quad 5 \quad \longrightarrow$$

So **X ≤ 1** means **X = 1** OR **X** is a <u>fraction</u> (e.g. **½**, **¼**, **1/6**, **1/8**, etc.), which means **X** is *smaller* (**<**) than **1**. For <u>fractions</u>, you just need to put ALL the pieces back together to get **1** *whole thing*. Below, **X ≤ 1** means **X** is a <u>fraction</u> OR number **1**. <u>Note:</u> To get **1** *whole thing*, fractions must be *positive*, so they can only be on the *right side* of *zero* (**0**).

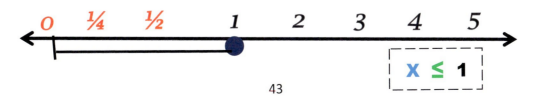

43

Note: *Negative* *fractions* *(e.g.* **-1/2**, **-1/4**, *etc.) always* add *(e.g.* **-1/2** **+** **-1/2***) to a number that's* smaller *than* **1** *(e.g.* **-1/2** **+** **-1/2** **=** **-1***), and* **-1** *is* smaller *than* **1** *because* **-1** *is on the* left side *of* **zero** (**0***). Individual* positive *fractions are always* smaller (**<**) *than* **1***. But if you* add *enough* positive *fractions, they will* equal **1** *(e.g.* **½** **+** **¼** **+** **¼** **=** **1***, just like one* **1/2** bird *+ two* **1/4** birds **=** **1** bird*).*

The fraction **1/10** *means* **1** whole thing *(e.g. an* apple pie*) was cut into* **10** pieces*. The numerator* **1** *represents* **1** slice *of the* **10** slices of pie*. What would you draw to show* **1** *whole pie* *was cut into* **10** slices*? Fantastic job! You drew:* **1/10** **+** **1/10** **+** **1/10** **+** **1/10** **+** **1/10** **+** **1/10** **+** **1/10** **+** **1/10** **+** **1/10** **+** **1/10** **=** **10/10** **=** **1**

The numerator **1** *in* $\frac{1}{6}$ *represents* **1** *piece of* **6** *pieces. When you* add *ALL the* numerators*, you get* **6/6***, which equals* **1** *whole thing* *(e.g.* **1** *whole pizza**). Now, what do you draw to show something was cut into* **5** *pieces? Correct! Wonderful job! You drew:* **1/5** **+** **1/5** **+** **1/5** **+** **1/5** **+** **1/5** **=** **5/5** **=** **1***.*

Note: *When you* add *fractions, you* total *the* **numerators***, but the* common **denomenators** do NOT change*! When both numbers are the same, you get* **1***.*

Instructions: Inequality Word Problems

On page 46, your child must figure out what Inequality sign *goes in the blank space between the letter* **X** *and the* number*. On a sheet of paper, have your child draw the following* Inequalities*:* **X** **____** **2;** **X** **____** **5;** **X** **____** **12;** **X** **____** **6;** *and* **X** **____** **4***. Then read the corresponding sentence to your* child. Afterward, ask him/her to draw the correct _Inequality sign_ on the line. Before all of that, you should review the data below with your child.

> | This symbol means "**bigger than.**" So an **X** value OR **number** on the _left_ side is _larger_ than a **number** OR **X** value on the _right_ side.

< | This symbol means "**less than.**" So an **X** value OR **number** on the _left_ side is _smaller_ than a **number** OR **X** value on the _right_ side.

≥ | This symbol means "**bigger than** OR **equal to,**" and means "**at least.**" So an **X** value OR **number** on the _left_ side is _bigger than_ OR _equal to_ a **number** OR **X** value on the _right_ side.

≤ | This symbol means "**less than** OR **equal to,**" and means "**at most.**" So an **X** value OR **number** on the _left_ side is _smaller than_ OR _equal to_ a **number** OR **X** value on the _right_ side.

Remember, the **open mouth (>)** always faces the **bigger** number. The line **(—)** under the _Inequality_ symbols **(≥)** and **(≤)** means _equal to_, just like the **(=)** sign. So the number on the _left side_ of the equal sign (i.e. **(=)** or **(—)**) must have the **same value** as the number on the _right side_ (e.g. **2 — 2** is the same as **2 = 2**; **7 — 7** is the same as **7 = 7**, etc.). The _symbol_ **≠** means the numbers on the _left_ and _right_ are **NOT** equal (e.g. 3 **≠** 4; 8 **≠** 10; 1 **≠** 5, etc.).

Inequality Word Problems

1. <u>At most</u>, Miss Smith gave **2** cookies to two visitors during lunchtime.

   X _____ **2**

2. Jason is <u>at least</u> **5** years old.   **X** _____ **5**

3. There are <u>not less than</u> **12** students playing outside.   **X** _____ **12**

4. There are <u>more than</u> or <u>equal to</u> **6** puppies in the box.   **X** _____ **6**

5. <u>Not more than</u> **4** frogs are in the pond.   **X** _____ **4**

Below are the correct Inequality expressions for the above situations.

1. **X ≤ 2**   2. **X ≥ 5**   3. **X ≥ 12**   4. **X ≥ 6**   5. **X ≤ 4**

Overview of Inequality Signs and Expressions

1. A **filled dot** ● under a number on a <u>Number Line</u> means the number is *included* in the **solutions** for **X**. An **open dot** ○ under a number means the number is NOT included in the solutions for **X**. The <u>Inequality expression</u> **- 7 ≤ X < 4** is shown on the <u>Number Line</u> below:

<u>Note:</u> *The Number Line* goes on **forever** in both directions. That's because you can always make a number **bigger** by *adding* number **1** to it (e.g. **10 + 1 = 11**; **-10 + 1 = -9**; and **-6 + 1 = -5**). To make a number **smaller**, you *take away* number **1**. To do that, <u>add</u> a negative **1** (i.e. **-1**) to a number. So **3 + (-1) = 2**; **-2 + (-1) = -3** and **-5 + (-1) = -6**. For <u>*negative numbers*</u>, the farther away from **zero** *(0)* a number is, the **smaller** it is. That's why **-8** is <u>smaller</u> than **-6**, which is <u>smaller</u> than **-4**. For <u>*positive numbers*</u>, the farther away from **zero** *(0)* a number is, the **bigger** it is. That's why **5** is <u>bigger</u> than **4, 3, 2,** and **1**.

2.   A **filled dot** with an *arrow* drawn in the <u>*rightward direction*</u> means the **solutions** for **X** are *bigger* than **or** *equal* to the number above the filled dot. The <u>Inequality</u> expression **X ≥ 2** *looks like this:*

-10 -9 -8 -7 -6 -5 -4 -3 -2 -1 **0** 1 2 3 4 5 6 7 8 9 10

3.   An **open dot** with an *arrow* drawn in the <u>*rightward direction*</u> means the **solutions** for **X** are *bigger than* (and do NOT include) the number above the open dot. The <u>Inequality</u> expression **X > 3** *looks like this:*

-10 -9 -8 -7 -6 -5 -4 -3 -2 -1 **0** 1 2 3 4 5 6 7 8 9 10

4.   A **filled dot** ● with an arrow in the <u>*leftward direction*</u> means the **solutions** for **X** are *smaller* than **or** *equal* to the number above the filled dot. The <u>Inequality</u> expression **X ≤ 7** *looks like this:*

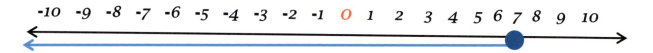

5. An **open dot** ◯ with an <u>arrow</u> drawn in the <u>leftward direction</u> means the **solutions** for **X** are *smaller than* (and do NOT include) the number above the open dot. The <u>Inequality</u> expression **X < 9** looks like this:

6. When **X** is <u>**more than**</u> OR <u>**bigger than**</u>, use this Inequality sign: **>**
(e.g. **X = 8** so **X > 5**, which means **8 > 5**, and **8** is <u>bigger</u> than **5** because **8** is <u>farther away</u> from *zero (o)* than **5**; **X = -1** so **X > - 3**, meaning **-1 > - 3** and **-1** is <u>bigger</u> than **- 3** because **-1** is <u>closer</u> to *zero (o)* than **- 3**.

7. When **X** is <u>**fewer than**</u>, <u>**smaller than**</u> OR <u>**less than**</u>, use this Inequality sign: **<** (e.g. **X = -7** so **X < -2**, which means **-7 < -2**, and **-7** is <u>smaller</u> than **-2** because **-7** is <u>farther away</u> from *zero (o)* than **-2**; **X = 1** so **X < 3**, which means **1 < 3** and **1** is <u>smaller</u> than **3** because **1** is <u>closer</u> to *zero (o)* than **3**.

8. When **X** is <u>**not less than**</u> OR <u>**at least**</u> a particular number, <u>**more than/greater than**</u> OR <u>**equal to**</u> a number, use this Inequality sign: **≥**

9. When **X** is <u>**at most**</u>, <u>**not more than**</u> as well as <u>**smaller than**</u> OR <u>**equal to**</u> a particular number, use this Inequality symbol: **≤**

About the Author

Dr. Courtney West was inspired to write *Princess Sasha Hides a Lion Family: Fun Algebra* after reading Dr. Keith Devlin's book, *The Math Gene*.

Dr. Devlin compared mathematical thinking to gossip. He suggested that Pre-K math education should be combined with stories that involve human interactions.

Princess Sasha Hides a Lion Family: Fun Algebra is the second release of a 12-book Algebra 1 series for children ages 4 and older. Upon completion of the series and its accompanying Practice Problems books, a 4-year-old child (after someone patiently reads the interactive books to him/her) should be able to solve all of the equations in Barron's *Painless Algebra* book, by Lynette Long, Ph.D.

Dr. West is the founder of www.sahasworld.biz. She has a Ph.D. in Mathematics Education and a J.D. emphasizing Juvenile Law from the University of Colorado - Boulder. Her B.A. degree in Journalism is from Rowan University of New Jersey. Dr. West resides in Centennial, Colorado.

Made in the USA
Columbia, SC
16 January 2024

29905383R00031